Woman on Canvas

Woman on Canvas

JESSICA RAMER

RESOURCE *Publications* • Eugene, Oregon

WOMAN ON CANVAS

Resource Publications
An Imprint of Wipf and Stock Publishers
199 W. 8th Ave., Suite 3
Eugene, OR 97401

www.wipfandstock.com

PAPERBACK ISBN: 979-8-3852-7498-7
HARDCOVER ISBN: 979-8-3852-7499-4
EBOOK ISBN: 979-8-3852-7500-7

VERSION NUMBER 03/09/26

Woman on Canvas is dedicated to the memory of Baruch Kimmerling, 1939–2007.

CONTENTS

ACKNOWLEDGEMENTS

"Sinner Woman." *Merrimac Review*, Spring 2015, no.3, p. 21.

"Bethlehem 2000." *Contemporary Haibun Online,* vol. 13, no. 1, 2017.Web.

"Stingray." *Haiku Journal*, March 2017. Web.

"Poems of Place." *South 85*, Spring/Summer, 2017. Web.

"Requiem for a War," *What Rough Beast,* August 16, 2017. Web.

"Skinned Knees," *Product,* no. 32, Spring 2018. Web.

"The Iceman's Route." *What Rough Beast,* January 31, 2019

"Reporting to the Armor Training Center." *What Rough Beast,* February 14, 2019. Web.

"The Last Prophet." *What Rough Beast,* February 22, 2019, Web.

"Knit, Purl." *What Rough Beast,* March 8, 2019. Web.

"ABCs of a Failed High School Teacher." *What Rough Beast,* March 15, 2019. Web.

"Outside the Sanctuary City." *What Rough Beast,* September 25, 2019. Web.

"Mash Note to Dostoyevsky." *What Rough Beast,* October 15, 2019. Web.

"Maxine in Alaska." *What Rough Beast,* December 19, 2019. Web.

"An Anonymous Road Worker Building Alligator Alley." *What Rough Beast,* January 18, 2020. https://www.indolentbooks.com/what-rough-beast-poem-for-january-31-2020/

WE DO NOT UNDERSTAND KOMEDIANTEN

Calvinism honed by frigid winters in Nova Scotia,
tar paper shacks, and potato suppers in Dust Bowl Kansas
methylated both our movie gene and humor gene,
switching them off unto the fourth generation.

Why else would my mother and I sit, puzzled,
watching *Annie Hall,* acclaimed work of cinematic genius,
dismiss it as an incomprehensible waste of money
better spent on squeaky toys for our dogs,

sheet music—her polonaises had separated
at the spine—or Legos for her grandson? At night, she recites
Wallace Stevens's poetry to me, becomes the book
as she had become her music while playing Chopin.

ODE TO MY FLUTE

For Fabiana Magrinelli Dahmer

My brother blows through soda bottles better—
you hear the notes—than I can play the flute.
I get the whoosh of air through a peashooter.

But after YouTube videos and brute
attempts to force blow hole and lower lip
together—my first sound!—a tinny toot,

one sure to make a concert flautist yip—
hands clapped on ears—at sounds like cracking knuckles.
I listen to beginner pieces slip

off key, each piercing shriek much like the scribbles
I call my poetry, their lines unfed
by melody, just desperate, plaintive warbles.

I ache, while joining body to the head
joint, for arpeggios and scales to prime
cascades of song, bore through the door a hundred

unuttered words have jammed, for tones to mime
those words I seek but almost never find,
bestowing music on each graceless rhyme.

WOMAN ON CANVAS

To near-sighted me, it looked at first like a frog:
its eyes those blobs of red inscribed in green—
that wooing frog had drunk too much persimmon beer—
gaping mouth the pale expanse between.

Glasses wiped and standing mere inches away,
I saw a half-naked form, her hair a tangled crown
falling ragged onto the threadbare blanket draped
over a woman too tired to put on a nightgown.

Multicolored orbs? Parts of furniture,
not amphibians. The pale patch? Thighs obscuring
parts fit for *Penthouse* and fleshy buttocks
bare above bent legs—intimate but unalluring.

This must be how others see me, I thought:
frizzed brown mane, unplucked brows patchy,
no amount of gray-covering dye and sunscreen evading
this human version of entropy.

Stiff and unsteady in the morning as if clamping
arthritic feet around a swaying tightrope,
I await—have I a choice? —that order emerging
like fractured patterns in a kaleidoscope.

REPLY TO ROBERT FROST'S "NEITHER OUT FAR NOR IN DEEP."

In black paper albums tucked between children's games,
Skeins of acrylic yarn, balls of crochet thread,
Forgotten family members rest, names
Unknown, each distilled to a dime-sized head.

We use wadded pictures of the Queen
To clean windows, crumple Wall Street kingpins,
Presidential candidates who preen
For cameras, drop them into recycle bins,

Yet keep unknown great aunts' photos, pore
Over Trilbies, bobbed hair, calico
Dresses, when failures unmoor
Life, melancholia whirls into vertigo.

If Frost had read evolutionary theory,
He would have known why men sit on sand
All day, turn bare faces to opaque sea,
Cotton-covered backs to dry land,

Watch ocean couple with sky from their quartz crust—
Because, once, water churned elements
Brought here on hot clouds of stellar dust
Into life—our half-remembered parents.

REFLECTIONS WHILE PLANTING A SPRING GARDEN

Her hand-sewn garment caked with loam and sweat,
Mitochondrial Eve sliced barley plants with a flint sickle,
flung them onto sun-faded earth, trampled them to liberate grain
from chaff. Man, freed by her labor from agrarian toil,
hunted and composed epics recited around nighttime fires;
she stuffed straw into the sleeping mat she shared with him.

Shoveling through knotted roots, compacted clay,
I have found kinship with my ancient forebear
whose loaves nourished children and grandchildren,
their descendants birthing women who fashioned
linen from flax retted, broken, spun, woven,
sewn into embroidered bridal veils or stark burial shrouds.

ON BUYING A TELESCOPE

Wrench my eyes from pixels on websites. Let me
Trace Orion's belt or the Little Dipper's
Handle pointing north as it beckons sailors
On the Aegean.

Let me see, not actors on screens, but Attic
Myths in night skies: Scorpio's tail, Aquila
Soaring next to Pegasus—ancient stories,
Poetry's cradle.

IMMORTALS BEHAVING BADLY

Nights on Mount Olympus where banquet tables
Groaned with sushi boats and carafes of sake,
Karaoke singers amused the gods by
Mimicking mortals.

When tempura ice cream was served, Apollo
Taught them scatological German phrases.
Ashen-faced Athena complained no goddess
Uses such language.

Zeus guffawed as Ares and Hermes spat out
Furz und *Scheiße*, guzzled Hokkaido-vinted
Ume wine while brooding Hephaestus taunted
"Hera's an Arschkuh."

Dionysus strutted in baggy trousers.
"Pull your pants up," Artemis ordered. "Gods look
Über stupid showing their undergarments.
Hybrid immortal!"

"Bite me, Virgin Mistress of plagues and hunters.
I don't care what celibate prudes who garnered
Goddess stripes defending uncultured Spartans
Think of my boxers."

READING ALL TWENTY-FOUR BOOKS OF HOMER'S ILIAD

Reading Homer's *Iliad* helped me see what
Dreams had shadowed. Bunches of bees—now grape-like
Clusters under flowering saw palmettoes
Pregnant with pollen.

Nameless birds—anhingas ensconced in mangroves,
Cocoa eyes surrounded by turquoise mating
Rings, extending wings to the sun as they dry
Ebony feathers.

But his epic stalls in a fifteen-book long
Saga of repetitive death as soldiers
Fall when speared through liver or groin, their bodies
Tossed onto pyres,

Names and hometowns set down in dactyls. Filling
Homer's endless litanies: aged fathers,
Greek and Trojan, left with no sons to pour out
Final libations.

At last, muscles knotted with ennui, I checked
Yet another book off my list of must-reads,
Thinking war a pottage of grueling boredom
Peppered with carnage
.

REPORTING TO THE ARMOR TRAINING CENTER

As our car wound down hills toward the troop train,
He grasped his mother's hand in mute farewell.
My wife betrayed the peace she hoped to feign

On hearing trumpets at the depot strain
To play God Bless America's last swell
As our car wound down hills toward the troop train.

Veiled hat obscuring brow and bark-grey skein
Of hair, pursed lips white as a sea-scrubbed shell,
My wife betrayed the peace she hoped to feign.

When he came home, we drove, deaf to inane
Tunes sung by soldiers drinking muscatel
As our car wound down hills toward the troop train.

Each time she helped him learn to walk again,
His new leg clattering each time he fell,
My wife betrayed the peace she hoped to feign.

Korea: we prayed for its end—in vain—
But sent a second son, knew he could tell,
As our car wound down hills toward the troop train,
We both betrayed the peace we hoped to feign.

CIRCUIT PREACHER'S WIFE

Six days she labored, my mother's mother.
For obeying the Biblical command,
she reaped forty dollars, women's wages.
Breast cancer, still in its early stages,
spun tangled webs through her chest as she penned
debits and credits in company ledgers.

And on the seventh day, with white-gloved hands,
she jolted with her husband, a minister,
over rutted roads to country churches,
where prairie winds blew organist's pages,
making her play ahead of the choir,
both enduring to their different ends.

They stayed for dinner in a sagging house
smelling like burning wood and coal oil.
Babies gnawed home-baked teething biscuits
while standing silently to serve her guests,
a stooped farmwife gummed a toothless smile
and smoothed her flour-sack dress trimmed with lace.

At home, the preacher's wife had time to slide
torso beneath water—her meager rest.
Jaws aching from pious self-restraint,
tired hands quivering from a day spent
obeying her God-given head in Christ,
she slept in her half of the marriage bed.

As a girl in buckled shoes, I forgot
my grandfather's prosaic cruelty
when I first sang Luther's and Wesley's hymns,
heard gentle cadences of the King James—
a Protestant child's first poetry—
trembling as ancient words filled ear and throat.

Now I recall, for my grandmother's sake,
poetry and cruelty grow in faith
like wheat and tares sown in the same ground,
laced at the roots, intimately entwined—
ineluctable truth leaving me both
doubting mystic and yearning heretic.

MAXINE IN ALASKA

[First Cruise]

Not quite twenty, she sails from Seattle to Anchorage.
Officers assign shipboard duties to military wives.
Her job: to balance on a rolling deck,
watch waves for Russian submarines.

[Anchorage]

False-front bars like movie set saloons
line pot-holed streets, their peeling paint
grey like tire tracks imprinted in melting snow.
On her first drive to the base, she brushes away tears.

[Base Roads]

[illegible]ed hands grip the wheel. She bites
her lip as she drives to work in darkness,
braking for stray dogs and moose.
Tires wrapped in snow chains slide on ice.

[Office Work]

Her boss, a bird colonel, suspends
sweet potato plants from his office ceiling.
She waters the only green she sees for six months,
stashes his brass watering can under her desk.

[Non-Commissioned Officer Meal Plan]

Moose meat simmers for days in her electric skillet.
Although it is tough and gamy, she welcomes
free food given by airmen hunting on weekends.
It supplements an enlisted man's meager budget.

[Homesteading]

Perched on cement blocks, a clapboard house
forms a den for a hibernating brown bear.
The animal stirs when children make too much noise.
"Shhh. You'll wake the bear," parents whisper.

[A Rumor of War]

Khrushchev bangs his shoe on the table at the U.N.
Elmendorf AFB prepares for war. Too afraid to go to bed,
Maxine falls asleep in her chair. At dawn, she opens one eye.
Then the other. She looks outside. There is still an outside.

[Heat Wave]

Summer sun lingers above the horizon past 10 p.m.
Starved for light after winter's darkness,
she stands outside in her magenta swimsuit,
plugs her iron into the porchlight socket.

[Twenty-one, Trapped, and Pregnant]

One week before her due date, March storms pile snow
chest-high
against the door. Shovel-wielding airmen dig her out.
She fears being snowed in when her baby comes. Jim Joyce says,
"Don't worry. If I can load bombs, I can catch a baby."

[Ersatz Milk]

Rows of blue and red cylinders fill the freezer—
condensed milk, cheaper than whole milk
shipped by barge from Seattle. Fifty years later,
she still insists the processed stuff tastes good.

[Winter]

Housewives bundled in parkas and galoshes
trudge across base housing's ice-coated quadrangle,
stop at Mary's house for their morning beer.
Darkness makes you drink more, they all say.

[Power Failure]

Electricity goes out—along with heat.
She bundles her children in snow suits,
takes them into bed—along with Yogi, the dog,
who bears the gift of body heat.

[Radar Operators]

Men posted to the archipelago of radar stations
facing Siberia descend on Anchorage for R & R.
Broken whiskey bottles litter downtown streets,
glittering in brief hours of daylight.

[Feral Dogs]

Pets abandoned by transferred owners
form packs roaming remote corners of the base.
Hunger lures them to apartment garbage cans.
Airmen hunt them down with Springfield rifles.

[Evacuation Drill]

Military wives and children ride in Army trucks
down gravel roads to a remote camp stocked with K-rations.
Canvas teepees promise privacy for latrine users—
until helicopters hover above open roofs.

[Spring Thaw]

A bear paces outside the city's only movie theater.
Dozens of patrons walk backwards through the doors.
Anchorage's one newspaper records the event:
"Bear Goes to the Movies." Which movie, it doesn't say.

[Maternity Clothes]

"Dan, hold the baby," she hisses at her husband,
who stares, unhearing, into the distance.
Her homemade maternity skirt falls off.
In church. On Easter Sunday.

[Christmas Eve]

Climbers disappear in the Chugach mountains.
Blinded by snow, the search and rescue plane's
pilot hits a slope, killing all aboard. Widows bear
cupcakes frosted red and green to the children's party.

[Border Crossings]

Inuits kayak across the imaginary line
dividing Russian and American waters,
trade seal meat, outboard motors, and furs.
Khrushchev and Eisenhower ignore this security threat.

[The Alcan Highway]

Pregnant again, Maxine bumps down the Alcan Highway in a
camper
reeking of propane and dirty diapers. Destination: Florida,
fresh milk, and cockroaches bigger than hummingbirds.
She arrives two months before the Cuban Missile Crisis.

MOVING TO FLATLAND

I used to live in Stowe, where maple leaves
Like paper hands with pointed fingers waved.
Aloft in autumn's gusty winds, they flew
Until they clothed nude hills in red and gold.
In winter, beeches bending under snow
Stood silent guard above our hockey games.

But then we moved to Flor-i-duh. Snow? No!
Six months of hurricanes. Instead of deer,
Iguanas rustling in Manila palms
Or hanging upside down above our door.
The beach? Watch out for sharks and men-of-war!
The Everglades? Mosquitoes! Gators! Snakes!

There's nothing good about this buggy place—
Except for dolphins leaping sea-to-sky
And greeting tour boats with blow-hole spray,
Anhingas drying damp wings in the sun,
Chameleons scaling walls with two-toed feet,
Pomelos plucked and eaten fresh from trees.

MY FATHER'S SOUP

Your room, only, was cooled. I often stood
by your closed door, my face pressed to the crack,
inhaling cold air, eyes raised, listening.
At noon, you emerged, made watered-down soup—
yellow water in a green plastic bowl—
which I ate, knowing not to ask for more.

But I, a child, always wanted more.
I raised the spoon to my mouth while you stood
before the sink, waiting to wash the bowl.
Bored, you smoked. I heard each paper match crack
and hiss before smoke wrapped you in gray soup.
Motionless, you eyed your china bear, listening.

At night, we both lay in bed listening,
Mother and I, to puffs of wind bringing more
heat, thickening that dank, sweltering soup
of a southern summer while trees that stood
in our yard swayed. Branches slapped with a crack
against dull paint chipped like a damaged bowl.

My brother dropped cigar butts in the bowl
where my goldfish swam, never listening
when I cried to see their dead bellies crack
sooty water, knowing I'd not have more.
A child wondering at death, I stood
staring as they floated in ashen soup.

Then you were gone. A new man came. The soup
had huge chunks of beef floating in the bowl,
served with a denied man's rage: mother stood
as he ladled it to me, listening.
Father, you always left me wanting more
but your inept love never left a crack.

Your brown china bear, still without a crack,
sits on my shelf, it's eyes clear as your soup,
steel blue, like ours. A whimsical piece, more
likely to preside over the punch bowl
than keep watch over a man listening
in the spare, ugly kitchen where you stood.

Last week, I stood as lightening slit a crack
through the sky, listening while I poured soup
in my bowl and thought *You, too, wanted more.*

DEGAS'S GREEN DANCERS

Clad in effusions
of tulle, we danced beneath trees
for men sucking pipes
clenched by tobacco-stained teeth,
eyes tracing our exposed thighs.

Smoke puffs ascended.
An arm, three stockinged legs formed
a diamond of flesh
pierced by a pink-slippered foot:
phallic flash lit by the moon.

TANKA

On reform school grounds,
railroad spikes welded by Scouts
into crosses stab
grass withered by southern sun.
Orange flags flutter over bone.

TOBACCO DREAMS

Staring at her image, he clicks his lighter,
Butane hiss made louder by hallway tile.
Smoke ascends. He struggles to reconcile
Love with no lover.

He returns her gaze from the wedding picture.
In her lace gown cut in that high-necked style
Common then, she stares with a distant smile.
She's for another.

Rooting through the hamper, he finds her panties
Buried under layers of children's Jello-
Spotted shirts, caresses its blue and yellow
Flowers, admits he's

No romantic rake—just an aging Don Juan,
Ready babysitter, a man to lean on.

MILITARY SCHOOL DOCUMENTARY

He clenches his jaws to damp tears.
Film clips show a few pooling above
lower lids. A ten-year-old "Piggy" lies marooned,
this time in an out-of-state military school
housing surplus stepsons and run by troop-to-teacher
marines. His matriculation papers were signed
by his newly remarried, now wealthy, mother.
"My parents sent me here and I'm trying to do
my best," he tells the interviewer. Already, he's learned
indifference is the best way to combat ridicule,
tucking in his shirt means he'll accrue
fewer demerits—and knows a mother's love
for fat boys ends when a new husband appears.

STATE ROAD 84

Running from ponds gouged in coral soil by bulldozers to water moccasin-infested sawgrass, State Road 84 bisects neighborhoods laced with Florida cracker boxes, jalousie doors bearing multiple decals proclaiming, "This is a Marine Family." One son comes back with surgical steel plates in his head. Julie, four years old, disappears. Neighbors suspect she was dumped in the Everglades by her mother's boyfriend. Women, neurons knotted by childbearing's hormonal tides, returned from the state hospital, skin yellow-gray and pacing compulsively from Thorazine. I Google them. The kid who poured gasoline on a snake and watched it writhe in its fiery halo appears in a booking photo, obese, teeth decayed, hair still long but greying. The lesbian dog groomer, the exterminator's son who became a chef, appear in reviews. Others leave no footprint in digital space.

In the east, dogs splash
in rock pits filled with June rain.
To the west, bones lie.

NAMING

"That fucking bastard!" reverberated from the backyard. The cat
lay stiff, blood foaming from its mouth, beneath the palm tree,
Running inside, the youngest thrashed air with fists, pretending, not to box
Alban, the presumed culprit, but to kill him. An eleven-year-old outlaw!
A preacher's daughter, she had wondered why children were called kids
instead of lambs. Then she heard that child's mouth.

At noon, after driving home past a "Put Some South in Your Mouth"
billboard, she tore stenograph paper, wrote notes about the dead cat—
"Show me you're growing emotionally," "Be mature," and "Big kids
don't get angry"—laid them out like first-grade Christmas tree
art, longer strips beneath shorter, breathing, "*Don't break the law.*"
Walking to her bedroom, she pulled money from her hair dye box,

slipped it into her purse. She found a teacher's note about a box-
and-whiskers plot, tossed it into the trash basket's overflowing mouth,
grabbed a card taped to her mirror: "Jeremy Smith, Attorney at Law"—
memento from a visitation suit. Outside, she pretended not to see Brandi, a cat-
house reject in fishnet stockings. An iguana climbed the ineradicable Florida holly tree
boys hid in while chanting "Fatty, fatty two-by-four," to the biddy next door. Kids!

At two-thirty, the ex-boyfriend picks them up from school—he always kids
the middle one about being fat. He pops into her life like a jack-in-the-box,
parks for hours next to his decade-old Easter gift, a poisonous tree—
who brings oleander to a woman with preschoolers? Head bobbing, mouth
twisting in a spurned man's rage, he plays the youngest like a bow on cat-
gut, stoking him to erupt like Old Faithful obeying some geothermal law.

A restraining order? Jeremy said he was rich enough to turn civil law
against her. His attorney will ask why she spent a decade exposing three kids
to a married man she now says is nuts, claim she neglects them to cat
around with her still-married boyfriend. In court, he will box
manipulated words into a transcript, its sworn, notarized mouth
spewing her private life to all when she wants to start a new family tree.

Mrs. Dix called. The middle one still didn't know how to form a factor tree.
Before dropping off food, she swung by the post office. The ex-mother-in-law
had sent the oldest a birthday card. That thin-lipped, colorless mouth,
false teeth clicking! She would hide the card in her closet while the kids
slept. Pulling into the driveway of her sun-faded Florida cracker box,
she edged past uprooted sod, a cardboard grave marker inscribed *Cavietta, My Cat.*

Tonight, she will eat at Kapok Tree Inn while a seminary student tells the kids
grace saves, but law condemns. Each will carry a Bible in a red box,
covers stamped "Jade," "Kirk" or "Zach," and mouth verses like a yawning cat.

STORIES OF SOLITUDE

Covid gels prison hierarchies. Lifers rattle with authority like pressure cooker valves. Inmates hoard commissary before the lockdown restricts canteen visits. Wardens suspend visitation, restrict access to JPay email kiosks.

Rats isolated in adolescence then returned to colonies react like prisoners released into gen pop after prolonged solitary confinement. Males roam, hyperactive. Female cortisol levels spike—after prolonged silence, being with others hurts.

Camus's Jonas craves both the lonely endeavor of art and time with his growing family. He retreats to his studio. On a canvas, he paints one word encapsulating his dilemma: The letter after *soli* and before *aire* could have been either a *t* or *d*. *Solitaire* or *solidaire.*

Thoreau gave us Walden, its pond described with a surveyor's calculation, a naturalist's descriptiveness, a flautist's music. He, too, blurred the *t* and the *d*. Solitaire in his cabin and jail cell. Solidaire with tides. Owls. Slaves. Invaded peoples.

.

Conrad's Savior of the Congo spurned *solidaire* with men who spoke his language, worshipped his God, swore obeisance to cousin-monarchs, yet turned back to enchant Congolese concubines and traders, depriving himself of *solitaire* and *solidaire.*

Had Kurtz possessed solitaire, he might have become Belgian Congo's Simeon Stylites, ensconced in a grass hut rather than perched on a fifty-foot pillar, a maggot-eaten eccentric memorialized in a Wikipedia stub.

Had he possessed solidaire with the woman whose bed he shared, he might have winced at white men believing themselves less savage than other savages—a truth Twain knew decades before Little Boy burst from Enola Gay's belly.

Instead, the diaphanous, European-tatted veil cloaking his savagery frayed, unraveled among men whose unknown tongue could neither mend this foreign covering nor garb him in one of their own making.

SKINNED KNEES

I cut the belly out of Kmart jeans,
Then stitched a spandex panel in its place
With thread I found in an old sewing case
Stacked high with *True Confessions* magazines.
I'll wear pink uniforms and sagging hose,
Get stiffed on tips by rich retirees,
Scrub diner highchairs caked with drool and peas,
Mom warned, and haunt thrift stores for baby clothes.
"It's not like running home with your knees scraped,"
Mom sobbed, then screeched, "You wouldn't flit between
Boys like a tramp—if you were really raped
At twelve—then come home pregnant at sixteen."
But girls cup palms around skinned knees and press
Because small pains make bigger ones hurt less.

TEENAGE APOCALYPSE

The four horsemen of the bitchy apocalypse—
Mom and I have our periods at the same time—
Usher in an ersatz family apocalypse.

The doorbell rings. "Nanny," with gray hair and wide hips
Looms. "Why do I have to call a stranger that name?"
Mom's four horsemen of the cranky apocalypse

Glare at me during dinner while pursing their lips.
"Nanny" snores on the couch all night outside my room
In a sleepless ersatz-granny apocalypse.

The next day, an unknown boy whose head's an ellipse
With acne—her grandson—dragoons me to his prom.
O four horsemen of the cootie apocalypse,

Deliver me from duty-date relationships.
Early next day, I lie, say I'm in love with him
And usher in a brimstone-y apocalypse.

"How can you be so selfish?" Mom yells as she whips
Her head around. "This could wreck my marriage. My home."
My four horsemen make her erupt in panicky yips,
As I usher in a mommy-apocalypse

EVERGLADES LEVEE BLUES

Cattails in the sawgrass, alligator eyes reflecting red,
Cattails in the sawgrass, alligator eyes reflecting red,
In his headlights, can't see nothing but loneliness ahead.

Hidden by the darkness, wary creatures stare at cars above.
Hidden by the darkness, wary creatures stare at cars above.
On stony levees, boys seek manhood and girls trade flesh for love.

I thought he loved me. Didn't even walk me to my door.
I thought he loved me. Didn't even walk me to my door.
Took off, rubber squealing. Won't think about me one second
 more.

Let me wrap myself around the body of my new guitar.
Let me wrap myself around the body of my new guitar,
Pretend I'll never be lonely when it makes me a star.

SINNER WOMAN

If I were a Holiness woman, my face would glow
With the peace of Christ as I clutched the belief
My daughter was in His arms after her brief
Months with me, knowing I would follow
Her as my old Sunday school fresco
Promised. Its pastel lamb motif
Mocks photos bound in a ribbon-tied sheaf
Taken months—and a whole lifetime—ago.
But I am a sinner woman mourning
My bastard child, her father unknown
Even to me, who watched the ocean stir
As the weighted urn sank, swallowing
An infant in an oyster-grey dress sewn
With faux pearls. I wear pearls at Easter for her.

SUGARCANE

He took his knife and pared the stalk away,
Revealing fibrous sweetness at its core
With hurried strokes because we could not stay.

Outside a house where gradual decay
Devoured buckled roof and sagging floor,
He took his knife and pared the stalk away.

Together by the grapefruit tree the day
Vacation ended, we mined sweetened ore
With hurried strokes because we could not stay.

As we watched birds in V-formation splay
Pale wings while traveling toward some farther shore,
He took his knife and pared the stalk away.

Before we left our adolescent play
For homes where no one met us at the door,
He took his knife and pared the stalk away.

South Florida's sunset mingling red and gray
Grew darker but because we wanted more,
He took his knife and pared the stalk away
With hurried strokes because we could not stay.

TOWARD A CITY OF REFUGE

Stars: jots penned in moonless ink.
My footsteps, tittles in shifting ink.

Alone, bedroll unfurled on sand,
I scribble mad woman's ink.

Dry loaves scrape my palm-leaf basket.
Waterskins crack, spill brackish ink.

Men suck last marrow from my bones,
Lick up stray bits of spongy ink.

The Virgin whispers "Go in peace,"
Words echoing in memory's ink.

Feet probe toeholds. Sweat and grit
Meld into canary-colored ink.

Lying in half-sleep, hair like cursive,
I fear shedding ink.

Acolytes' mythologies persist
On vellum stained with gall-nut ink.

Note of grace: galaxies expand,
Write my life in vanishing ink.

ON DEPRESSION

After I had shivered and wept in Hades,
Choking down libations so vile none but
Pluto, Lord of Death, could esteem them honors,
Hermes snatched me

Back to Mount Olympus and banquet tables
Heaped with lamb. Elysian fires warmed me
As Apollo plucked his enchanted lyre,
Notes like nectar.

Fragile comfort, feasting with gods and drinking
When the scarlet seeds in my belly send down
Stubborn rootlets ferrying me back over
bitter waters.

THE LAST PROPHET

To Israel Shahak, of blessed memory, chemist, human rights activist, and Holocaust survivor

When I was a girl, I watched a man—
the ersatz father—as he watched
prison movies: unfortunate women
were stripped of their clothing,
shorn of their hair as he stared,
his voice vibrating with choking, sexual joy.

But when you came to me, they came to me,
characters, a whole cast of them, women
brought forth by you, clamoring to be heard,
who spoke what I dared not speak myself.

The Mathematician

The more one learns, the happier he becomes.

Not happy, but happier.

In the realm of nothingness,
numbers reign, an anodyne;
in their austere beauty,
eternal truth
revealed in a two-line proof.
It's easy. See.

The Mystic

I don't know if God exists, but if he does, it is my duty to oppose him on human rights grounds.

Years I looked for you without knowing you—
among wary-eyed guest workers in Berlin,
indigenas in Guatemala, blank-faced as soldiers,
rifles at ready, ordered them off the bus.

When I found you, in a chain restaurant
outside New Britain, tenuous enlightenment
unraveled into soft, dark clots and I stood mute.
The gifts I had brought you seemed intrusive
as a catheter, trivial as a laundry list.
Instead, I gave you the gift of silence.
You gave me a voice, this two-edged thing held close.

The Mourner

One of the most stupid myths is that victims become better through their suffering.

When I awaken in the middle of the night,
the first thing I hear is the sound of your voice
as you forced yourself to sound pleased,
trying and failing like a drunk trying to light
a cigarette but without the comedy.
Before, I would have lain awake in silent tears,
but now, like the elder in Dostoyevsky's novel,
I bow before you in silence, forehead on the ground.

.

The Prostitute

Humiliations are worse than shootings. To beat a man in

front of his children is worse than shooting him.

Stop trying to prove something to me.
You are insulting me.
Do you think by criticizing the prime minister
and the Rebbe that they—whoever "they" are
next time—will say, "He is one of the good ones.
Let him live"? Do you really expect goodness
to count for so much? How many troops does
the Pope have and would he use them to help you?
The answers are none and no. And the old black hat
is dead, so let him rest in peace.

And yet, I remember sitting in an outdoor cafe,
before I had hardened myself into the mold
of my new life, as you took the teapot
from my trembling hands and poured for me
as though serving an honored guest.
That is why, although I could never believe in you,
you remain the man my thoughts return to when I am alone.

To wish you happiness is cruel,
so I wish for you what you can have:
rage that binds your broken voice together
transporting you past barbed wire fences
to good meals and sound sleep.

The Mute Girl

Justice cannot be divided. Either there is justice for everyone or there is justice for no one.

Freed of that gauzy veil of words swaddling sight,
The mute girl sketches the prophet in deft strokes
as he plucks a Beilstein from the unruly heap
of books in his travel bag. Her drawing peels off
intellectual detachment, reveals the prison-cast calm,

shadowed eyes, and that slight asymmetry
beaten into children who have known hunger.
He glances at her drawing: she sees
what he does not as he trims his mustache in the mirror.
He gazes off into the distance and nods, almost imperceptibly.

But this mute girl would hope
the rebbe you despise is right:
may his god in whom you don't believe
and in whom I don't believe
send you tumbling back—for the joy
it is your task to obtain, to sing in your unbroken
voice and write the poetry stolen from you.

ON THE BERLIN U-BAHN, 1985

When I returned to say my last goodbyes,
My body swaying as the U-Bahn rolled,
I saw a man with prison in his eyes.

He held his dog as if to exorcise
Some desperate sorrow festering unconsoled
When I returned to say my last goodbyes.

The train pulled in. I left in chilled surprise,
But as the station's escalator scrolled,
I saw a man with prison in his eyes.

I strolled the Breitscheidplatz where Turkish pies
And t-shirts stamped *I heart Berlin* are sold
When I returned to say my last goodbyes.

Outside its bombed-out church where scaffolds rise
Like bars, the Savior's visage in their hold,
I saw a man with prison in his eyes.

Inside that cage, a one-eyed Jesus, wise
But distant, called his lambs back to their fold
When I returned to say my last goodbyes
And saw a man with prison in his eyes.

(PRAY, FAST)

She tossed her journals in the trash, debris
Acquired plotting sacred algebra—
Prayers in her heavenly language the abscissa,
Long fasts the ordinate of ecstasy

She never found. Her quest for piety—
No swimsuits, splashing in the sea, gardenia
Corsages for school dances, their aroma
Suffusing braided hair, just Bible study—

Reminds her of those parallel lines deft
Rotation of her compass, slant of ruler
Created on erasure-smudged graph paper.
However long she drew them both, the cleft
Between her segments stayed the same, with each
Adjacent and yet always out of reach.

WOMAN WITH ASHES IN FRONT OF MARJORIE STONEMAN DOUGLAS HIGH SCHOOL

Fresh ashes crossed on her forehead proclaimed "believer." Yet, as she stood with her arms around another mother, each waiting for her child to emerge, hands in air, she must have asked why. Her bishop had told her God grants free will, not knowing—or perhaps knowing but not saying—that will plays in time with football concussions, combat injuries, and psychiatric drugs propelling troubled men out of depressive chrysalides and into gun shops hawking AR-15s.

I find it daunting to believe when mind clog dances to neurotransmitters. Maybe our only freedom is to choose, or reject, Him. Or maybe only those who inherit the god gene choose him. Church fathers have long taught that faith is a gift. We know, now, this gift comes wrapped in alpha helices.

Branching like dendrites—
cypress trees where egrets roost,
heads tucked under wings.

KNIT PURL

Jitterbugging all night to Benny Goodman's swing,
His wife flushed as stocking tops showed under maroon
Taffeta folds whirling in time to "Sing Sing Sing."

The band struck up "Moonglow"; they swayed in a cocoon
Spun by their arms. He breathed with her, inhaled her scent—
Their steps keeping time to the alto sax's croon.

Demobbed after the war, Farsleben, two months spent
Lugging Belsen's still-dying survivors—that girl
Who smiled at him—to the white canvas morgue tent,

He sat in the dark, would not look at sheets unfurl
On clotheslines, hunched when wooden knitting needles thunked
Like dirt shoveled on a mass grave. Scrape. Thud. Knit. Purl.

TO AN ANONYMOUS ROAD WORKER ON ALLIGATOR ALLEY

"Please Lord, I've been a good man. So if I get cotton-mouth bit, or attacked by some of Oscar the Alligator's brothers, and if I get to that Big Job in the Sky, oh, please, Lord, let it be on dry land. Amen!" [1]

You stood in swamp water up to the knee,
Muscles moving to the rhythm of space,
Toiling to build Alligator Alley.

Within that sawgrass curtain where wary
Denizens guarded their kingdom of space,
You stood in swamp water up to the knee.

Stripping off muck as your walkie-talkie
Chattered, you slogged through this bedlam of space
Toiling to build Alligator Alley.

Imprisoned by miles of sawgrass sea,
And yearning to flee this "freedom of space,"
You stood in swamp water up to the knee.

Far from home, you prayed, "Let my next job be
On dry land, not some two-bit thumb of space,
Toiling to build Alligator Alley."

Nameless man, known only by a scrawled plea
In an outhouse squeezed on some crumb of space,

1. Graffiti on an outhouse for the Alligator Alley road crew quoted in bassonline.com

You stood in swamp water up to the knee
Toiling to build Alligator Alley

MASH NOTE TO DOSTOYEVSKY

Turgenev called you the nastiest
Christian he had ever met.
Critics despised your pious
submission, not knowing
our prisons are coiling gyri,
the very stuff of God.
We must submit.
At the Siberian *katorgi,*
floggers plied their trade, spoke,
voices choking, of their calling,
swallowed saliva as other men do
when talking about cunt.
Flayed by Siberian hell and divine
epileptic ecstasy, you had no skin,
throbbed like a five-foot abscess
of interictal irritability.
Yet, I loved you after your first
twelve sentences, studied Russian
to roll your words over my tongue,
created dialogues for us because
you knew. You knew.

CHRISTMAS EVE, 2000

Childless at forty, I crossed from Jerusalem into Bethlehem to mark the birth of another woman's baby. December rain, two checkpoints, and a newly birthed Intifada had left Manger Square empty of all but men in rough woolen robes, white-haired women in gray veils, and me, in Israel to meet an illicit love, swaddling our virtual affair, at last, in flesh—our own incarnation, the Church of the Nativity a mere side trip.

In the grotto, I watched celibate women worship a virgin's son, their faces immobile in meditation, and wondered if they, too, were forcing themselves yet failing to feel the presence of the Christ child and dreaded going home to a spartan cell and narrow bed.

After sixteen years, I remember less a peasant baby placed in a feeding trough than an unknown mother's teen son manning a checkpoint. Bundled against the cold, Galil slung over his shoulder, he handed my passport back to me through an open taxi window and wished me a Merry Christmas in my own tongue.

on frigid hillsides
soldiers, Gregorian chants
sound in counterpoint.

ARTEMIS AT 15

The moment I turn off my bedroom light,
She limps across my faded faux-wood floor,
stares out smudged windows, and barks at the night.

I nudge arthritic legs—she tries to bite
now if I grab her collar—through the door.
The moment I turn off my bedroom light

—again—she bangs her water bowl to fight
off sleep then, disobeying me once more,
stares out smudged windows and barks at the night.

No longer wedging frail hindquarters tight
against my knees before she starts to snore
the moment I turn off my bedroom light,

she sleeps apart, or with her failing sight
and deaf to pleas to cease her graceless score,
stares out smudged windows, and barks at the night.

I, with arthritic spine and shrinking height,
know why this greying cocker troubadour
—the moment I turn off my bedroom light—
Stares out smudged windows and barks at the night.

BUZZWINKLE'S APRIL ODYSSEY

Headlines called him the smartest moose
Alaskans ever saw--
Crossed streets when signals changed to green.
That old bull knew the law.

One spring, he'd eaten last year's grass
Before new growth came in.
Game wardens winced to see the beast's
Hip bones against his skin.

He sauntered amid lilacs wrapped
In holiday displays
Sun-starved men left to brighten up
Long months of dusky days.

All twigs devoured, he ignored
Stares of suburbanites
As he walked off, his antlers hung
With strings of Christmas lights.

Before retreating to the woods,
The grazer stopped to scrounge
Last summer's unpicked fruit outside
A false-front Anchorage lounge.

The moose pawed snow, found frozen spheres
Dropped from tree limbs last fall,
Not knowing late year heat ferments
Crabapple alcohol.

By his twelfth helping, hooved legs locked,
He turned a glassy stare
Toward soldiers shaking off the cold
Inside their yeasty lair.

When Ranger Rick came out, he did
What men do when friends quaff
Too many beers on Friday night—
He let him sleep it off.

That night, a desperate journalist
Confronted with a dull
Day wrote about the drunken moose
She christened Buzzwinkle.

The photo shows his six-foot rack
Festooned with filaments
Cascading down both massive sides—
To his indifference.

That cruelest month, birds and stray dogs
Stalked round him when they spied
A fallen moose, hooves tracing arcs
In air while on his side.

Rick swore Buzzwinkle never saw
Him aim or felt the shell
That pierced his skull but with its flash,
Four legs grew still and fell.

The mayor said their town had lost
Its best ambassador
But ten years later, he lives on
In sourdough folklore.

ON BEING FOUND BY A FIRST COUSIN

I signed and spit to let technicians trawl
Pyrimidines and purines—ancestry,
Disease risks, both revealed for a small fee,
Test tube replacing cards and crystal ball.

I thought of photographs stashed in our crawl
Space—traces of forbidden family—
When I read my allele chart. This is me:
Teutonic, double-dose Neanderthal.

With email. When our genomes matched, she found
Me, missing half a century, a stranger
Attached to distant petiole but bound
Together by an alpha-helix tether.
We typed, deleted, typed as we unwound
Long muffled words—my cousin, our grandmother.

BALLAD OF A SNAKE-HANDLING PREACHER

Glenn lived beneath a railroad bridge
Near Thatch where he was born,
Slept in a leaking canvas tent,
Ate parched, unsalted corn.

His daddy owned the biggest still
In rural Tennessee.
He drove a brand-new Cadillac
While Glen ate hominy.

His mama wed a sinner man
Whose friends spent life knee-deep
In whiskey and shot two men dead.
Glenn feared to go to sleep.

Octobers, Glenn worked sun-to-sun
In browning cotton fields.
Each year the tired soil gave
Stooped pickers smaller yields.

When Glen was twelve a desperate man
Evicted from his land,
Discharged his Colt, hit Glenn who held
His insides in his hand.

He thought he saw a coffin lid
Slam down on him that night,
But then he heard the voice of God:
"My son, you'll be all right."

The Holy Ghost surrounded him
With God's paternal love.
He felt the shield of faith descend,
Protection from above.

When he was grown, his Daddy said,
"Come help me make moonshine.
We'll sell these bales of weed I've got.
Us two can live just fine."

That money bought a great big house
High on a mountain side.
The lure of riches ruled his life,
And not Christ crucified.

When sadness gripped him, Satan said,
"Son, go and get your gun,
Then put the barrel in your mouth.
One pull and then it's done."

God spoke, said: "Put away that gun."
Obeying Him, Glenn flung
That rifle down. The spirit fell.
He got his heavenly tongue.

He burned his pot and sold his house
Then bought a single wide
Back home in Alabama where
He walks by Jesus' side.

Within a year, he heard God say
"Do this for Jesus' sake:
Go find a church that works the signs;
Take up a rattlesnake."

The Holy Ghost surrounded him
With God's paternal love.
He felt the shield of faith descend,
Protection from above.

He works the nightshift in a mill

Alongside his new wife.
When he comes home, he prays in tongues,
Thanks God for his new life.

He tells the crowds at county fairs
"Friends, sin makes you a slave,
But God our loving father sent
His Son to heal and save.

"And then he'll send the Holy Ghost
To comfort you with love,
And you will feel the shield of faith
Protect you from above."

HAIKU

Stingray flap on leg
Clamoring word dreams smothered:
In silence, I see

IN THE GARDEN OF NO LANGUAGE

Turnip seeds small and dark as graphite pencil leads spill onto soil. Two months later, a thicket of greens chokes rain-eroded ground from which white and violet bulbs protrude.

Parsley seeds remain dormant. Carrot seeds produce stubby orange growths six months after planting. But seeds scraped from kabocha guts and tossed on the compost pile explode into vines laden with heavy squashes. Japanese radishes erupt in raised beds.

Gardens bestow a comforting aphasia. No words to tug into poems or shoehorn into articles.

Alone among my plants, I let language lapse, touch what I bring forth.

Under autumn skies,
Lyrate daikon leaves rustle.
Roots pierce clay soil

A FORMER STUDENT'S SENTENCING HEARING

Other women sitting on bare wooden benches,
polyester tops snagged from too many washings,
must have thought I belonged to the blond man—
drawn face and hunched posture branding him "Addict"—
while I was that white trash mother who had poured
Mountain Dew instead of milk in his sippy cup.

But I belonged to Jackson. Or his name had once appeared on my class roll. Hinges squeaked as I passed through the wooden gate separating convicts' women—and we were all women— from lawyers, judge, and court reporter in their padded chairs. Her Honor cast a hard, sideways glance at me, clearly not the defendant's mother, yet too middle-aged to be a young man's lover.

At school, I had been hit by hurled books, pelted with black-eyed peas, but Jackson greeted me with "Good morning, Miss." A flawed lineup convicted him, I told the judge. Jackson alone wore short dreads. He stood for his sentence: twenty-five years. She did not add "Good luck to you, sir," as she had with the others. A uniformed man rolled his prints, led him out a side door.

DRAFT DODGERS OF CHEROKEE COUNTY

When Woodrow Wilson sent doughboys
To string up Kaiser Bill,
His agents raided slackers' farms
In Georgia's red clay hills.

Old men who'd watched Cump Sherman march.
Swore to their tight-faced wives
By Jesus they would never let
War blight their grandsons' lives.

They hid their kin on untilled land
Right outside Harmony.
As younger boys stood watch, girls brought
Ham hocks, grits, and sweet tea.

A preacher riding through pine stands
Heard rumbling, saw truckloads
Of soldiers, spurred his piebald horse,
Took off down unpaved roads.

Sharecroppers grabbed arms and handsaws,
Flowed down in human streams,
Merged at the Etowah's main bridge,
Cut through its aging beams.

As tires rolled across the deck,
It buckled. Men with guns
Forced open metal doors, pulled out
Imprisoned, war-bound sons.

Three privates died—all immigrants—
In uniform because
Sweatshops left them too poor to buck
Old Weasel Word's draft laws.

Investigators knocked on doors.
Conspirators all swore
Those piers were weakened by that blaze
Cump set in sixty-four.

ABCs OF A FAILED HIGH SCHOOL TEACHER

For Darius

Afraid of getting kids beaten, I never call parents. The ruckus is audible throughout the hall. A student wraps metal in paper, lobs it at my head. Two hours later, my scalp still stings. "We didn't tell you this because we didn't want to scare you off," a teacher tells me, "but you have some bastards in your classes."

Brian winces when I ask my class on the first day if anyone wants to be a teacher. "Miss, if I couldn't make it as a bum, then I would try teaching." His reason: "If I was a teacher, I would kill those kids. If I killed them, I would go to prison. I do not want to go to prison. Therefore, I will not be a teacher." QED

Chronically short of markers, teachers run out before the first term is over. I buy my own. "Never spend your own money on school supplies," my boyfriend tells me. "Ask for paper instead of plastic at the grocery store. Clip the bags to the board. Write on them with charcoal scrounged from grills at the beach."

Daily flag salutes precede announcements broadcast over CCTV. My classes never see them—I won't incite patriotism and encourage enlistments. Once, I had to let my kids watch. Thirty ESOL students—Haitians, Brazilians, Mexicans— jump up, hand over heart, and recite the Pledge of Allegiance from memory.

Enlistees during my last year: Alberto, my best algebra student, who wants a fast track to citizenship. Randy, Anglo, fatherless—his remarried mother signed for him. Diego, perpetual troublemaker I spend every class trying to shush. Each will be issued an M4 carbine and deployed to Bagram or Baghdad.

Fist in air, Pierre yells, "Sue Ellen, I'm going to have sexual intercourse with you until your genitals fall off." Anyone who works with teenage boys will recognize this as a paraphrase. Instead of calling security and having them removed, I make them apologize. When I collect his paper, Pierre whispers "I love you, Miss."

Gwen, an unmarried guidance counselor, knocks, asks if she can tell my kids about the PSAT. A recruiter hiding behind the door enters, tells them the army will pay their college tuition, swears he can keep them out of combat. I tell them if they enlist, they will fight in Iraq, not study in Florida. I wait to be turned in.

Holding his Nokia,Daniel says, "You can use my phone. I'll even dial the number for you." I had threatened to call home after he had thrown books, dropped trousers, and paraded in boxer shorts. He punches in the number. Grandma speaks only Creole. I say, "Daniel a jeté des livres dans la classe." His eyes widen.

In a geometry class, I prove that the measure of an exterior angle equals the sum of two remote interior angles: $m<1 + m< 3 = m<4$. An administrator, a former band director, enters,thinks I am teaching them $1 + 3 = 4$. He points to the board. "This is spoon-feeding!" Someday, he will have a street named after him, I fear.

Jackson, a star football player carries a backpack with "Real N---a Shit" written on the back in black marker. Gang violence kills two friends. Years later, prosecutors charge him with shooting an unarmed Haitian teen. The victim lives. Jackson gets a 25-year mandatory minimum. I wish he had enlisted.

Kids can't add three-digit numbers without a calculator. I forbid their use. Anne screams, "The school lets us use calculators for the FCAT. Are you better than the school?" "As a matter of fact, I am," I reply. She stares, lips parted, not knowing Bart Simpson's "I am so great" theory of American social relations.

Larry burbles with joy over the invasion of Iraq, happy as a kid who just lost his virginity to the head cheerleader. "I teach my students how to pay for college. I've brought in recruiters from the Army, the Marines, the Navy, and the Air Force." A recruiter asks him to join. He responds, "Are you crazy?"

Memorized multiplication tables, knowledge of fractions, grade-level reading ability: all MIA in this school. Pictures of our mascot, a buck, hang in a school serving a mostly African American population. Posters encourage good performance on the high stakes test required for graduation. "Buck the FCAT."

"Novels are books with two hard covers," the reading coordinator tells us during a meeting which consumes our entire planning period. We grade and plan at home for free that night. *Newsweek* places our school on its list of the nation's top four hundred schools nationwide, she says. The faculty response? A very long silence.

Oranges, cake, candy, and soda sit on my desk, party food for the last day of school. Tenise frowns. "We don't deserve a party. We're a bad class." I stand in the doorway, monitoring the hall. The tardy bell rings. Turning around, I see the Gang of Four—Freddy, Tales, Jimmy, and Daniel—hurl fruit across the room.

Pierre falls to the floor, clutching his groin. "She hit me in my balls. She hit me in my b-a-l-l-s," he groans, elongating one syllable into three. "She" was Sue Ellen. I hope the principal does not walk in. That night, I do not sleep well: If Pierre hits Sue Ellen, he will be led away in handcuffs.

Quarters and Quartiles dominate school life. A fourth-quarter loss in the game's last second kills playoff hopes. The bottom quartile of students fails to make sufficient academic gains. We remain a D school. Our principal hires a consultant who spends six hours lecturing us on how to teach strategic guessing and back-solving.

Relationship etiquette is MIA, too. Two students French kiss in the last row. She dumps him. He punches another kid. She takes him back. He tattoos her name on his bicep. She gets pregnant—at fifteen. He disappears. "My pregnancy was a mistake, but my baby is a gift from God," she tells me.

Student graffiti: American-born kids scribble slang for intimate body parts using substances the color of feces. Immigrants chalk parodies of school life. "Fight: Sue Ellen vs. Pierre. After school on the football field. Free tickets." A Brazilian student writes, "Jesus died for you. Respect that."

Teacher Appreciation Day posters invite us to lunch. *Isn't it nice of the administration to do this?* I smile benignly at my administrator-nemesis. But it was army recruiters offering hot dogs and potato salad in exchange for access to our students. Mr. Cohen tells them he will never agree to it. I remain silent.

Underwear displays are a thing here. Manuel stands in the back, lifts his shirt, revealing sagging pants and oddly cut briefs. I almost say "Mr. Gonzalez, your underwear is completely old-fashioned and out of style," but didn't. They were not American, one of the few things he still owned from his country.

Vandalism—someone wrote that a student was "a bout it ho" in the girls' bathroom—causes the principal to ban bathroom passes. Students wait for security guards to escort them. Kids with long after-school bus rides beg me to break the rule. I do. I never knew this girl's name but I still think about her.

Word walls, once confined to first grade, sprout up in our D-school classrooms. I create placards: *Parallel, Perpendicular, Obtuse, Acute.* Some student pencils his own word wall: the S-word, the F-word, the N-word, the MF-word. I point to it. "This is disgraceful." Years later, I still admire the kid's gift for parody.

Xenophobia bubbles like an air pump in a fish tank. A student writes male names on the board. "Dexter, you can't write the names of your 'homeboys' in geometry class," I said. "That's 'neighbors' to us," a white kid blurts out. Students stare at desktops. I write James Garfield's proof of the Pythagorean Theorem.

Y?—textspeak for why. Why must Rosa wait two years to be evaluated for learning disabilities? She drops out, surrenders her dream of an army career. Why does Jean-Claude's father shave his head as punishment? I report it. The one thing I do right in years of failure. He comes by every day to give me a hug.

"Zo-zo. Zo-zo. Zo-zo." Walter's off-key singing continues for three days. Zo-zo. Zo-zo. Zo-zo. Finally, I ask, "What does zo-zo mean anyway?" A student points to her lap. "It's this, Miss." Creole slang for the penis. I still love every kid in the class for not laughing at me. Zo-zo remains the only Haitian Creole word I know.

"You see Jesus in the faces of the poor," the pastor said. But he gives sermons to old ladies and had never taught in a Title I school. On Friday, I yell at Anthony for telling me I do not teach well. Monday, I apologize. He looks puzzled. "What for?"

Xenomorphs—strange shapes, not space aliens—draw groans from students. "Miss, is this FCAT? It looks like FCAT." I say, "Find the area of an irregular polygon by dividing it into regular ones. "We already took that test." They tell me the exam acronym stands for, sort of, "Forget College After This."

Waving a belt yanked from his trousers, Walter slaps it across a desk, missing another student. Barely. I have him removed from class. The next day, a Creole-speaking teacher's assistant and I meet with his stepmother, tell her how much we like Walter, how much he wants to help. We hope his father will take it easy on him.

"Vote for Bush-Cheney." Eric, named class clown by graduating seniors, enters my classroom on election day waving a yard sign bearing the candidates' photos. "Tell your parents to do the right thing and vote for Bush-Cheney." He grins at me, knowing I have a Kerry sticker on my car bumper.

Uniforms for the band and flag team sprout mildew after a summer of improper storage in Florida's heat and humidity. Parents can't afford to buy new ones. The county won't allocate the money. Kids who had enjoyed flashy red and gold jackets now wear white tee-shirts with the school logo on it.

"The Tent is just like school only you sleep there at night," Marlow said, using the nickname given to the county's juvenile detention center. "You go to class just like you do here." I email the story to Baruch. "What a nice compliment for the school," he responds.

Students too poor to afford winter coats walk to school wrapped in tattered blankets. At my mother's school, they wrap sheets around their arms. Below-freezing temperatures cause cold-blooded iguanas to become insensate. Newscasters warn Floridians to beware of iguanas falling from trees.

Recruited by top colleges, two football players win four-year athletic scholarships, their escape from poverty. Failing FCAT scores block graduation. Three times, they earn a 1, the lowest score. The fourth time, they earn a 5, the highest mark. A much brighter Haitian girl fails English by two points, sobs in class.

Quadratic equations mystify students. Parabolic curves—free throws, Hail Mary passes— nothing connects. They drown me out with an explicit discussion of ano-genital activities. I put down my marker. "You have a choice. You can discuss quadratic equations or sex." A minister's daughter says, "Miss, you're crazy."

Poker mania sweeps campus. Kids smuggle playing cards in their backpacks. Chris, who has not brought a pencil to school all semester, now brings several to tally wins and losses. He settles up after school. Plausible deniability: if I do not see money change hands, I cannot write him up for gambling.

Oceans churn with hurricanes that year. Wilma knocks out electricity, closes the school for two weeks. On their return, kids write me notes. "I have not had a hot meal in ten days. My stomach hurts." "I listened to my cassette player. Then the batteries ran out. I need light. Help. Help. Help."

Noise levels exceed workplace safety standards. One morning, first block students talk so loudly my ears ache until the next day. I refer unserved detentions to the behavior specialist. They remain in his mailbox untouched. Girls removed for disruption ask to be taken to him.

Maury Povich wannabee Marlow wads unfinished work sheets into a microphone, pretends to emcee a paternity-test show. Daniel plays an accused father. I paraphrase: "She had sexual intercourse with my best friend. She had it with my brother. She even did it with my pastor. And she say's I'm the father?"

Lockdown begins after the war starts. No hall passes may be issued for any reason. Kids who need to use the bathroom must wait for ninety-minute classes to end. "Miss, nobody needs to bomb this place," Sue Ellen (who else?) tells me. "This place is ugly enough already."

Kids sit in class and cry after a three-day weekend. Keith Jenkins had been shot to death outside a convenience store on Dixie Highway. Years later, I see his picture, recognize him as the kid in dreads who had walked past my classroom every day, drawing eyes to him as he smiled, imbued with life.

Jean, a Haitian immigrant, slumps to the ground, shot in his front yard when he steps outside. Airlifted to Broward General Hospital's trauma unit, he recovers—after doctors remove so much of his large intestine that this kid who loves food must eat saucer-sized meals for the rest of his life.

I am warned that my job is in jeopardy if I don't keep my classes under control. When a boy ties another student's shoelaces to the table leg, I call home. The kid's face contorts as he listens. When the call ends, he buries his head in his arms. "Miss, he's going to get a beating tonight," a girl tells me.

Haitian Flag Day prompts fears of ethnic tension. Seven sheriffs' department cars park around the rear of the school. More gather near the main entrance. The day passes without incident, we think, until we learn that an American student had been gunned down weeks later for burning a Haitian flag in the school parking lot.

Graduates sit through the pledge. Stand when they are supposed to sit. Refuse to shake the principal's hand. Boo administrators. Parents laugh, proud of their kids' defiance. They are protesting their school's failure to stem tensions leading to off-campus murders of three students.

FCAT day arrives. Math teachers should have taught their classes all the tricks advised by that consultant during a six-hour meeting. If a non-multiple choice problem involves a geometric figure, students should draw that figure on the test sheet. It shows some understanding of the problem and raises the school's score.

Edric arrives from Haiti, saying, "No English." Even algebra teachers must have reading periods. A school-supplied book about the civil rights movement uses a racial epithet. I stop reading, not wanting his third English word to be that one. Rouldy, almost fluent, raises his hand. "I'll read it for you, Miss."

Ducking out of class without permission. Donald returns, finds I have locked him out. He peers through the glass partition on the left side of the door. Other students laugh at his woebegone expression as he jiggles the doorknob, eyes pleading to be let back in. Teaching, I tell my students, is more entertaining than TV.

Carpet patched with duct tape decorates upstairs classrooms, its soiled blue clashing with the mottled green board serving as a fourth wall. It can be pushed aside, providing an extra escape route during a fire. A student artist chalks a few quick strokes, drawing a naked woman. From behind. Bending over.

Black-eyed peas ricochet off classroom walls, hurled by students who had brought them from home. Eric tosses one at me and laughs. Security comes. So does the principal, who sits in the room throughout the exam. My brother tells me I will laugh about it someday. Someday has not yet come.

"Asshole! Asshole!" Darius yells when the administrator leaves the room after reprimanding me for sitting while taking roll. The man returns. "I can hear everything you say." He leaves. "Asshole!" Darius shouts louder. The next day, I say, "Darius, about yesterday. Thank you for supporting me."

REQUIEM FOR A WAR

Kyrie

Lord, teach me when to draw my sword.
Christ, teach me when to sheathe my sword.
Lord, have mercy on me: teach me to beat
my own sword into a rototiller and trowel.

Dies Irae

Dies Irae: *March 17, 2003*

St. Patrick's Day parades wind through American streets.
Bush's war deadline passes. No fighter planes shriek above
Baghdad.
America threatens like a man jingling his belt buckle
for hours while his son trembles in the bedroom.

Tuba Mirum: *March 18, 2003*

In the Boratha cemetery, a man in patched white trousers
recites
ritual chants over four new graves, voice rising and falling
rhythmically like a wind instrument. He earns a few dinars
for each body.
Between prayers, he looks up, listens for bombers.

Scriptus

October 2002:

It is written in the book secured by armed guards outside a
Senate office:

Iraq does not have weapons of mass destruction. Six
senators read it.

March 2003:

"Read the Koran, Mr. Bush," an Iraqi American said, "and
may God
not curse you for what you have done to our people."

Quid Sum Miser

March 19, 2003: Bombs loaded with chemical gels ignite
beams.
Children shriek for mothers pinned beneath fallen roofs as
flesh, hair, bone
return to the carbon cycle, a sacrifice for Tigris-watered
soil
rendered barren by depleted uranium unto the fourth
generation.

Rex Tremendae Majestatus April, 2003

Saddam Hussein flees. In Queens, mosques fill with his
exiled victims—
men bearing the preternatural calm and deep eyes of the
tortured,
women weeping over mummified sons in desert graves.
"God has answered our prayers." The man standing in
Boratha Cemetery chants over seventy fresh graves.

Recordare, Late 2003:

Kalashnikov-bearing extremists drag Iraqi Christian
women into the streets, beat, rape, and sell them.
On Christmas Day, worshippers leave a Catholic church
secured

behind blast walls, barbed wire. Car bombs explode, killing
twenty-six.

Ingemisco, August 2003

"I wish I knew another language fluently, like German,"
my brother told me as we sat in the Mikado eating sushi.
That way, if I go abroad, I could speak German
and no one would know I was American."

Confutatis May 2004:

A teenager arrives at a Fallujah military hospital, legs gone,
testicles shredded, penis hanging by a flap of tissue.
Genitals thud into the medical waste container.
Surgeons perform twenty genital amputations that month.

Lacrimosa:

Women disfigured by war live childless and celibate.
In Fallujah General Hospital, Rashil gives birth to her first
child, a son.
His face is misshapen. His brain juts outside his skull.
"Depleted uranium," she says, weeping.

Domine Jesu

May their dead and our dead
nourish their native soil.
May our maimed and their maimed
find a place where no eyes slide away.

Hostias

Lord, in praise of those men and women
who sacrificed themselves for us, I offer

nineteen dollars a month and the proceeds
from my garage sale to a veterans' charity.

Sanctus

"Mom. Mom. Mom! I want some drinky stuff."
Cum laude graduate in biology, he lies in bed, optic nerve
severed, neocortex pierced by shrapnel. His mother comes
bearing a lidded cup and aluminum tubes of useless balms.

Benedictus

Every Fourth of July, Baruch greets me:
"God save America." The Bush administration
boasts that our military owns Iraq's air space.
He emails, "America save God."

Agnus Dei

Archeologists sifting with brushes and sieves unearth a
civilization
possessing bronze scythes but no swords. A vanished people.
Genghis Khan survives in the millions spun from his alpha
helices.
Lord, our DNA cries out to You: teach us to beat our plowshares
into F-16s.

Lux Aeternum

Give us light according to our portion and no more.
Grant darkness to Gitmo inmates bathed in perpetual brightness,
sun to those detained in darkness, noises muffled.
Let us all see the moon as if for the last time.

Libera Me

A story from another conflict: a Filipina surviving war and occupation
stocks her American basement with sixty-pound bags of rice, gallons of fish sauce,
screams at her misbehaving child, "I wish I'd died during the war than have a daughter like you."
Her daughter does not know where wars end, only how long they last.

READING *ADAM BEDE* IN MOROCCO

Marrakech cafés where I gamely mangle
"Je voudrais du thé"—the djelabbahed waiter
Standing, pen suspended in air—and splutter,
Bruising each vowel,

Summon girlhood memories of Brownies' apple
Bobbing contests, coming in last when water
Swirled stemmed spheres much faster than I could skewer
Teeth through their mantle.

Adam Bede, his gift with no need to call on
College French, Larousse as my shield and broadsword,
Sates like fresh-baked bread in an aching gut cored
Hollow by famine,

Feeding me, a rootless and tired woman,
Dinah's compassion.

PARSIMONY OF NATURE

Delta of Venus, whose heroine painted
her vulva red with lipstick as men's breath quickened,
has been placed on the closet shelf holding
other books that will never be read again,
along with postcards from the Lothario I mistook for a lover.
One mailed from the Mediterranean
reads, "Next October, we will be here together."

I should have known I was merely a stop on his flight
from the aging wife he denied having,
two bookies dunning him for money he owed.
But I saw this only after a hormonal bender
subsided into an aching middle-aged hangover,
and the sensuality I tried to conceal but couldn't quite
manage to do, he said, faded like ink on an old love letter

COMPENSATIONS OF AGING

Pompano Beach's industrial section, a variegated jumble of cement block
structures spewing black smoke from roof tar, dust from buffers
shaving tread—reverberated with curses of men loading tires
onto trucks. It seemed no place for two nuns garbed in ancient
habits. "Pray this and you will become a Catholic." A blue paper,
medal glued to it, held a prayer. Her smile did not extend longer on the left.

As mine does. I recited the Hail Mary. Still Protestant, I left
trinket and prayer in the beer tray I won after buying a block
of raffle tickets, a receptacle for scraps of paper
too small to file yet too important to toss, nail buffers,
letters from Wanderjahr men who were not quite ancient
history. I did not yet know how memory both torments and tires.

Saturday, Catholic kitsch still on my desk, I read the article "Bishop Retires."
In his last interview, he proclaimed celibacy a gift, a sentiment that left
me thinking "I hope no one ever gives me a gift like that." When I'm ancient,
I'm going to spend my last days with younger men, not in some block-
like modern church with hymns and incense serving as holy buffers
against death and a mirror reflecting skin mottled as the browning paper

filling my grandfather's *Harvard Classics* or that August 1974 paper
bearing the headline "Nixon Resigns," one given to me in 1982 while buying tires,

cheap newsprint crumbling in my hands. Contemplating this old
scandal buffers
against the dread of being incarcerated, manless, with battleaxes
left
by impatient families at senior citizen condos. I bought sunblock,
SPF 100, loaded with avobenzone so I wouldn't look ancient.

Even when I was. Now I am—at least to my students—ancient.
Hormones that churned emotions into whirlwinds like tissue
paper
shredded and spun aloft by Category 3 hurricane gusts have
evaporated, no longer block
everything but desire. I have withered into Yeat's rooted truth: life
attires
its young in beauty; I have shed my lying leaves yet rejoice to have
left
behind a diet of uncooked need garnished with numbness,
fleeting satiety as buffers.

During that Wanderjahr, Fritz read my palm. His words have
served as buffers
against decades of chaos. Although his prognostications echoed
ancient
proverbs, not prophecy, they grew true. With time, I have indeed
left
adolescence and young adulthood tumult behind, have learned to
paper
over losses with a cribbed joy—lacking youth's fire but one that
never tires--
in saltwater nudging sand, waxing moons—a calm merciful as a
saddle block.

Once *eros* left, indifference to its absence a gift, I no longer
needed buffers--
Like calcium leached from crumbling bones—to block still-
throbbing, ancient

hurts picked at the way toddlers tear peeling wallpaper until even raging at faithless lovers tires.

www.ingramcontent.com/pod-product-compliance
Lightning Source LLC
LaVergne TN
LVHW020654100826
845148LV00012B/2480

* 9 7 9 8 3 8 5 2 7 4 9 8 7 *